IT'S NOT GOD, *It's Me*

A BELIEVER'S GUIDE TO OBTAINING THE PROMISES OF GOD

This 30-day devotional is curated to bring transformation, revelation and results to the believer. It's specifically tailored to the woman of God who is waiting on a promise from the Lord and has been waiting for what seems to be an extended amount of time. This devotional is curated for the woman of God who finds herself battling fear, doubt, or insecurities when it comes to stepping out in faith. She has a vision of what she wants her life to look like, but year after year, she's no closer to achieving it. This devotional is for the woman of God who is ready to team up with God and walk into everything that God has for her. In order for us to walk into the promises of God, we need to be able to navigate this thing called life with God being our GPS while staying the course! This devotional will help you to understand how God works, so you can team up with him!

To experience real transformation in as little as 30 days, set aside a designated time to complete every activity in this devotional Daily. Just because life has always been this way doesn't mean it has to stay this way. It's time to walk into your abundant life.

"Now unto him that is able to do exceeding, abundantly above all that we ask or think, according to the power that worketh in us."
Ephesians 3:20 KJV

Contents

Day 1
Purpose In the Storm

"Remember how the Lord your God led you through the wilderness for these forty years, humbling you and testing you to prove your character, and to find out whether or not you would obey his commands."
-Deuteronomy 8:2

I remember going through a very difficult season a few years back. What made it so difficult was the fact that I had no one to turn to. Why? Because during that time, everyone I trusted was saying the opposite of what God was telling me. It wasn't until I broke down asking the Lord *'why are you allowing me to go through all of this? Why can't you tell at least one person what you're telling me so I don't feel so crazy?'* He responded in my despair, because Dennisha, where I am taking you, I need you to listen to me even when everyone else is saying otherwise. It was at that moment I realized God was cultivating in me resilience and obedience to Him regardless of the circumstances or judgement from others. So that when He brought me into the promise, I would have the resilience and obedience needed to maintain and sustain the promise.

We have a tendency to lose faith during seasons of trials and tribulations. Not realizing that those seasons are key to developing us into who we need to be to carry the weight of the promise that we are destined to walk into.

This passage of scripture is a loving reminder of how God is not only concerned about our current well-being but our future success as well. Jeremiah 29:11 is an example of that as well. God, our Father, always has the end in mind. To bring us to an expected end, to a hope and a future. For I know the plans I have for you," says the Lord. "They are plans for good and not for disaster, to give you a future and a hope (Jer 29:11).

Have you ever taken a moment to ask yourself what did the last season of my life teach me? How did I or should I have grown from it? How can it benefit me in the future?

Take a moment in prayer and ask the Lord, what was He trying to cultivate in you last season? What is He trying to cultivate in you this season? Journal your discovery here.

Day 2
The Power of Knowledge

Hebrews 10:36, 38-39
"You need to persevere so that when you have done the will of God, you
will receive what he has promised."
Hebrews 10:36

If it wasn't for God revealing to me what He was doing in that difficult season, I would not appreciate it as much as I do. The knowledge of God's will in that season allowed me to shift my perspective, stand on God's Word, and team up with Him for the manifestation of my future, my expected end. Without the knowledge of what God was doing, I would have started to doubt whether or not I was hearing God, start to question my motives, and ultimately make the wrong decision.

When we know God's will, it empowers us to persevere. Often-times, we put our will above God's will. But only 'God's will' will get us into the promise land. If the promise is the destination, then God is the GPS.

So the question is, do you know God's will? Because Hebrews 10:36 says when you have done the will of God, you will receive what He has promised. One definition for 'will' is: The thing that one desires or ordains. The will of God is the predestined desire of God.

Take a moment to pray this prayer:

Father, as I continue to wait for that which you have promised me, I surrender my will to yours. In this moment, I ask, Lord, that you will reveal your will to me so that I may come into alignment with it. For your Word declares that only then will I receive the promise. And because you honor your Word above your name, I stand in faith that *I SHALL RECEIVE EVERYTHING YOU HAVE FOR ME. IN JESUS NAME, AMEN!*

Day 3
The Power of God's Word

Psalms 138:2b

"for your promises are backed by all the honor of your name. " NLT
"for thou hast magnified thy word above all thy name." KJV

The day I realized I was tying God's hands behind his back, I was in prayer, and I started to pray for the finances of the body of Christ and myself. During that prayer, I brought God's Word back to his attention. (YES! I get bold like that in prayer) I said God, you honor your Word above your name and your Word says that the wealth of the wicked is laid up for the righteous. God, I want to know why do they still have our money? I was not ready for, nor was I expecting the answer He gave me. The Lord responded, " because you're wasteful." Wait what? So, it is my fault? Since then, the way I read God's Word and my level of obedience to it has never been the same.

We have a tendency to take one portion of God's Word and start decreeing and declaring it all over the place. Not realizing that because God is a holy God who cannot lie, He can't honor one portion of his Word while dishonoring another portion of his Word. We have to be a good steward over the little that we have so God can honor his Word and make us rulers over much (Matt 25:21).

Because God honors his Word above his name, once we come into alignment with his entire Word concerning anything, we will begin to see the creative power of God's Word. It immediately goes forth to do what He has sent it to do.

Take 20 minutes and pick one thing that you are waiting on God for. Open your bible app or download the "you version" bible app and type that desire into the search bar. Study the scriptures that relate to what you are asking for. Determine what areas you are strong in and what areas you need to work on. Take this revelation to the Lord in prayer and have a sincere conversation with the Lord about where you are falling short. (Ex. finances, wealth, money, marriage, wife, husband)

Day 4
The Power of Surrender

"For I have come down from heaven to do the will of God who sent me, not to do my own will."
John 6:38 NLT

I remember this one time the Lord instructed me to do something very specific. It was not something that I wanted at all, I knew what the end would be, and I really didn't want to do it. But I love the Lord and I trust him, so I was obedient anyways, despite my desires. I did exactly what he told me to do. Based on what he told me, I thought I knew exactly what the end result would be. I surrendered to it and laid down my will for God's will. But when things didn't work out the way I thought they would, I went back to the Lord in prayer. I said Father, you are an omniscient, all-knowing God. You know everything before it even happens, so if you knew that things would end this way, why did you tell me to do this? The Lord responded to me and said Dennisha, my Word did exactly what I sent it to do. The problem is people don't always know what I send it to do. You made the assumption of what the end result would be, but that wasn't my intention. I didn't like the way God brought about the end results, but I did love the end results. It was something that I had wanted for a long time.

The 'will of God' is the predestined desire of God. The Word of God is the command that brings that will/desire/promise to pass. Jesus is the living Word of God, and he says in this particular verse that he has come down from heaven to do the will of God, who sent him. "Not to do my own will." Think of it this way, During the creation in Genesis, God desired light (His will), He said let there be light and there was light (His Word). Why? Because the authority of His Word has creative power.

God makes His will known to us by sending His Word. So why isn't His word "creating" and bringing His will (our promises) to pass in our lives. There are several reasons why. But I'll just mention a couple here.

- ▲ #1 We are not fully aware of what God sent His Word to do. The scriptures say we know in part and we prophesy in part (1Cor 13:9). The fear of the unknown causes hindrance in our obedience.
- ▲ #2 We haven't surrendered our will to the will of the father. Jesus came in the flesh and was surrendered, submitted, and obedient to the Word of the Lord. His will was to do the will of His father. Jesus was the living Word wrapped in flesh.

God's Will is a creative force, and our will is also a force. If those two forces are opposing, creating resistance, then the creative process cannot take place because God will not force his will onto us. This is the reason why there is power in our surrender. The more we surrender, the more God's will can be revealed to us. Our surrender must be followed by submission and obedience.

Surrender - Cease resistance and submit to authority.

Submission - Accept or yield to a superior force, authority, or will of another person.

Obey - Comply with a command and submit to the authority.

Take a moment to Process:

Concerning the promises of the Lord, in what areas have you not completely surrendered your will to the will of the father?

Day 5
The Power of Vision

"Write the vision, and make it plain upon tables, that he may run that readeth it."
Habakkuk 2:2 KJV

My back was against the wall, and I was being forced to make a decision I did not want to make. You see, I was accustomed to only working Mon-Fri because I had devoted my Saturdays and Sundays to the Lord. Because of that, I had made tremendous spiritual growth. I could see where God was taking me, and I was excited. But the job I was working at for 5yrs put out a notice requiring all employees to start working weekends. I immediately refused, and they gave me all sorts of weekend options. But, you see, I had previously made a vow to the Lord that my weekends were His. Plus, I had a vision of where I was going and working weekends were not a part of that vision.

One day on my way to work, knowing I was at risk of losing my job I started to doubt my decision. I thought about the fact that I had a kid to feed and not much savings. Then the Holy Spirit said to me, what can separate you from the love of God? My answer, Nothing! In that moment, I put on my big girl undies and stood my ground, kept my vision in sight, and did not sacrifice it. The next Monday, they told me Friday would be my last day of full-time employment with them. I was scared, but the very next day,

I received a job offer that I never applied for, that was 10x better, and I didn't have to work weekends.

We have a tendency to lose faith when everything starts to go wrong. If we can't cultivate the ability to see past what we see, we will never be able to believe what God is asking us to believe.

Vision has the ability to decide for you what needs to be done even if it's a decision your flesh doesn't want to make. Have you ever been presented with a difficult decision and you did not know what to do? Next time, ask yourself this question. Will this decision take me closer to my vision or farther away from it? Will it take you farther away from God? If you find yourself justifying your answers then you're probably leaning into the wrong decision, the decision that would please your flesh more than it would glorify God.

What is your vision? Let's jot one down now! What are you waiting on God for? How will you feel when you receive it? What will your life look like? What will change? Who will you have to become to maintain and sustain it? Be as detailed as possible.

Day 6
Now Faith

---

*"Now faith is the substance of things hoped for, the
evidence of things not seen."*
Hebrews 11:1 NLT

Doctor: Based on what you're telling us there's no reason you
shouldn't be able to have children.

We'll run a few tests....

Unfortunately, ma'am, your tubes are blocked, and we couldn't
clear them.

Me: Both tubes?

Doctor: Yes ma'am, both tubes. But don't worry, we can do
IVF.

We'll just have to do an ultrasound first....

Unfortunately, ma'am, even if your tubes weren't blocked, there
would be nowhere for the egg to implant because you have a
large fibroid right in the middle of your uterus.

Me: So, what your saying is I have my very own birth control
factory going on down there.

Doctor: Yes ma'am, but don't worry, we can do surgery to remove it.

Me: OK!

Doctor: We just need to get you scheduled and do some Pre-op blood work....

Unfortunately, Ma'am, we have to cancel the surgery.

Me: Now what?

Doctor: Well, you're severely anemic and your blood count is so low you would never survive the surgery....

I could go on and on! But here's the thing, I have a vision of holding my own child in my arms and she looks just like me. So, I prayed one last time and the Lord told me, "NO SURGERY, I will do this." Then He Gave me a diet plan.

A divorce and 5yrs later, the fibroids are degenerating (losing oxygen and dying off), shrinking, and evacuating my body. *Faith is the substance of things hoped for, the evidence of things not seen.*

Our faith is the proof of the things we don't see (in the physical realm) being convinced of their reality even though we don't see the manifestation of it.

Have you ever had your faith tested to the point where you started to get mad or disappointed at God? Like He was letting you down? If we are honest, we've all been there. God has the ability to configure a better plan even when ours don't work out.

Take a moment to pray this prayer:

Father God, I may or may not know the reason for the delay of what you have promised me. But today, I choose to activate my "NOW FAITH."

Right NOW, I believe!

Right NOW, I have faith!

Right NOW, I can see it!

Right NOW, I can feel it!

Right NOW, I promise to believe in what I do not see until I see what I believe. Father God, I know you are a promise keeper. And you will keep your promise to me. In this, I have my faith.

In Jesus Name, Amen!

Day 7
Active Faith

"faith, if it does not have works [to back it up], is by itself dead [inoperative and ineffective]."
James 2:17 AMP

When the first follow-up ultrasound revealed that the fibroids had grown, I could have been tempted to give up on the diet plan that God gave me. But then, that would have been the true measure of my faith. I could say with my mouth that I have faith that one day I will have children. But by itself wouldn't be enough. My level of faith is proved by my level of action. Therefore, I decided to believe and have faith in the report of the Lord. It may have taken longer than I desired to see the results of my obedience (5yrs). But not once have I been deterred from God's diet plan. And I won't until I see the fruit of my womb. Why do I still believe after so many years and no husband in sight? Simple, because God said it. And He's a holy God incapable of lying. So, in the meantime, my nephew, who's under my care, I treat him as my own!

Our faith tends to be verbally active and physically passive. And according to scripture, that means it's dead! Maybe we get a prophetic word, a vision, a knowing of what God wants to do. We get excited about it. We might tell a few people. Then we do nothing, we sit, and we wait. Not realizing that there's the part that God does, and then there's the thing He wants us to do. That thing might be to wait, but there is such a thing as actively waiting.

Are you believing God for a financial increase? Then apply for that promotion!

Are you believing God for a new car? Then work on your credit score!

Are you waiting on God to save your husband? Then treat him like he's already saved.

Write a list below of something you can do to actively demonstrate your faith.

Day 8
The Power of Obedience

He replied, "Blessed rather are those who hear the word of God and obey it."
Luke 11:28 NIV

"Now then, my children, listen to me; blessed are those who keep my ways. Listen to my instruction and be wise; do not disregard it. Blessed are those who listen to me, watching daily at my doors, waiting at my doorway."
Proverbs 8:32-34

I remember going into prayer to the Lord in this one particular season because I was frustrated. The Lord had asked me to build something for him. And as I started to gather all the tools and materials I would need, I started to get overwhelmed because the building of this thing required me to gather a lot of information. I was reading four to five books at the time just so I could build this thing. I was so overwhelmed with the magnitude of the work that I started to experience mental fatigue. I prayed, and I said God, I'm overwhelmed this is too much. The Lord responded to me in that season and said to me Dennisha, you're overwhelmed because you didn't do what I told you to do last season. I told you to read those books last season, but because you didn't read them, you have to be learning and building at the same time this season. When I realized it was my own fault why I was overwhelmed, I repented, and I asked God to grace me to finish well because I refused to stop just because I was overwhelmed.

We have a tendency to give up after we have stepped out on faith because of the different circumstances that arise and cause us to get frustrated and overwhelmed. It's imperative that we remain obedient in every season. Why? Because each season of our life is connected to the next season. What we don't do this season will affect us next season.

Even though I still pushed into the next season, even though I didn't get everything right in that season, what is important to know is that some seasons are prerequisites for the next season. Meaning if we don't complete everything, we will not be able to enter into the next season until we complete the current season. It's the same thing with some courses in college. Anatomy & Physiology 1 is a prerequisite to Anatomy & Physiology 2. Which means you're not allowed or eligible to register for A&P 2 until you take and pass A&P 1. When this happens, we find ourselves and our lives going in cycles where it seems like our life is stagnant and we are being hindered in certain areas of our life.

Have you ever felt like you were stuck where no matter how much you prayed concerning something, it didn't change? You know what God has promised you concerning it, but you just don't seem to be making any progress toward it. It's because you are stuck! There is something that is a prerequisite for you to progress into the next season, but you haven't done it.

What is it that you haven't been obedient in? What have you started but never finished? What is the Lord trying to cultivate in you because you're going to need it before you can receive the promise? What is the prerequisite?

Take a moment to pray this prayer:

Father God, you told me/revealed to me ______ (what God promised you) ______, and it has not come to pass. God, I know that according to your Word in 1 Samuel 15:29, you are not a god that you should lie, nor a man that you should change your mind. God, if I am the problem, then please reveal to me what I need to do on my part so I can team up with you in every season of my life. Lord, I truly believe that your Word concerning my life will not return to you void, so please instruct me in accordance with your Word. In Jesus name I pray.

Expect God to answer you, then obey!

Day 9
The Power of Devotion

But seek first his kingdom and his righteousness, and all these things will be given to you as well.
Matt 6:33 NIV

But without faith it is impossible to please him: for he that cometh to God must believe that he is, and that he is a rewarder of them that diligently seek him.
Hebrews 11:6 KJV

The one thing I learned early on was that if I truly wanted to grow personally and spiritually, I needed to spend time developing an intimate relationship with God. I knew that if I wanted to do that, I had to spend a lot of time in prayer, worship, and the Word. I called this my time of devotion with the Lord. It was during my times of devotion that I would hear the Lord speak to me the most. It was during those times when I would develop strong convictions that I was determined to honor. It was during devotions when the Lord would give me instructions and provide clarity that would strengthen my faith in him. Obeying those instructions led me into the most blessed seasons of my life.

If we are trying to get to the place where God promised us, and he's the only one that knows how to get us there, then we need to constantly be in communion with him to get those instructions.

We have the tendency to pick and choose which instructions we're going to follow depending on our comfort level. But the reality is all the instructions are needed to get us to our destinations. Think of it this way. If you plugged an unfamiliar location into your GPS and then ignored the directions, would you ever get to your destination? No! Then why is it that we think we can still make it to the promised land while ignoring the instructions God is trying to give us? It's easy to ignore the instructions when you feel like completing it is outside of your capacity. But it's in those moments that you have to remember that it was God who made you, and he knows what you're capable of even if you don't know. Stop downplaying what you're capable of just because you've never been told just how amazing you really are. It's easy to ignore the instructions when you realize worst case scenario can possibly affect your livelihood. But the truth is your identity rests in the fact that you're God's daughter and everything he does is perfect. This means when you trust and obey him, you never have to worry about the worst-case scenario because, with God, every scenario ends in success. Have you ever disregarded God's instructions because they were uncomfortable? Have you ever avoided spending time with God because you were afraid of what he might say and instruct? Have you ever kept praying about something even though you knew what God was saying, but it wasn't what you wanted to hear?

Take a moment to pray this prayer:

Father God, I repent for not diligently seeking you, for your words declare that you are a rewarder of them that diligently seek you. Please forgive me for not being obedient to your instructions because I know that you have my best interest at heart. Lord, please help me to learn how to rely on your instructions and your wisdom and not rely on my own understanding. Holy Spirit, please lead me in the way that I should go and strengthen me to do the things that I should do. That I may seek God's face and not his hand. In Jesus name I pray, Amen.

Navigating The Silent Seasons

"When you make a vow to God, do not delay to fulfill it. He has no pleasure in fools; fulfill your vow. It is better not to make a vow than to make one and not fulfill it. Do not let your mouth lead you into sin. And do not protest to the temple messenger, "My vow was a mistake." Why should God be angry at what you say and destroy the work of your hands?"

Ecclesiastes 5:4-6 NIV

Before I started my own business, I was working full-time as a nurse. I had no desire to start a business, but God had other plans. It was January 2021 and the COVID vaccine had just rolled out. I remember being in prayer and I vowed to the Lord that I would not take the vaccine until he revealed to me that it was OK for me to take it. As a nurse, I knew it interacted differently in certain individuals. I also knew only God could be 100% sure if it would adversely affect me. For eight months, I prayed that prayer, but the Lord did not answer me. Then the vaccine became mandatory for healthcare workers, and I began to pray more often. Because I worked at a big organization, I didn't have to worry about deciding quickly. Then a series of divine events took place that got me red-flagged with health services at work. Ultimately, they said I had to get the vaccine, or I could not work there, along with other threats. Because God still did not answer me, I submitted my resignation without having another job lined up. Why? Because I refuse to allow, man and fear to force me into breaking my vow to God. The very same evening I submitted my resignation, I got a job offer for a job I never applied for (for the 3rd time). Then 2:30 the next morning, I woke up to use the bathroom and when I returned to my room, I felt the peace of God fall on me like never before. It was so overwhelming. I said, God, what is this? He responded the vaccine; you can take it. I was so shocked "God, why didn't you tell me this yesterday before I quit my job." He said, "because if I would've told you before, you would never have left the job." He was absolutely right; I had no desire to leave my job. God purposely forced my hand, gave me a part-time job, and told me what my purpose was and the business to start. It was my obedience in the previous silent season that set me up financially and that's what allowed me to work part-time, all seasons are connected.

The most difficult season that we go through as believers is the silent season. This is where God has gone silent, and he is not speaking during a time when we need him the most. This is where the convictions you develop in your devotional time comes into play. The silent season comes right before the new thing God wants to do in your life. And when you navigate it well, you will walk into a blessing you never saw coming.

But it's the silent season that tends to take you out, because fear and doubt kicks in during the long periods of silence. To navigate the silent season well, you must honor your convictions regardless of the circumstances and consequences. If God can trust you to honor your convictions, he will use those same convictions to help you to make a decision you wouldn't normally make. It's in the silent season when God will close one door and open another. You will know that the closing of a door is God because the only way you can keep it open is if you dishonor the convictions/vow you made to the Lord. When you honor your Word to the Lord, He, in turn, will Honor you!

Take a moment to think.

What are some of the things you told the Lord you will or will not do? Write them down. If a time comes when you have to choose between honoring what you said to God or break it, take the leap of faith and honor it. God has something great in store for you.

Pray this prayer: Lord, I trust that you are guiding me even in the silent season. I believe that you are my shepherd, your rod and your staff truly comforts me. Help me to stay true to my relationship with you, that I would honor the words I utter to you, so you can use them to guide me in the silent seasons. Help me, Lord, to identify when my seasons are changing and when you are trying to do a new thing. Lord, I promise to trust you even in the silence. I will trust your heart even when I can't trace your hand. In Jesus name I pray, Amen.

Day 11
The Power of Submission

The Lord directs our steps, so why try to understand everything along the way?
Proverbs 20:24 NLT

Your plans for us are too numerous to list.
Psalms 4:5

I have a friend. Let's call her Nicole, who is the go-to person for everyone. She knows what she wants and knows how to get it. She has a very independent mindset, and everyone comes to her for help. Nicole is the rock of her family and when everyone is falling apart, she cannot fall apart. She has to be the strong one for everyone else. If Nicole does break, she does so privately and very few people will know when or if she is going through something. Nicole is the dependable one. I like to call Nicole my blueprint sister! Why? Because she is the one who always wants the blueprint from the Lord. Before she steps out on faith, she wants all the details before she obeys. The reason Nicole does this, whether she likes to believe it or not, is because she wants to be in control. It's what she's accustomed to in all her other relationships. And if she wants anything done right, she often has to do it herself. One of the things Nicole struggles with is staying the course that God puts her on. Because when things start to go wrong, she switches gears and takes matters into her own hands, going into full fix-it mode, straying from God's original course, not realizing that God has already accounted for the things that are going wrong. Afterall, God is all-knowing!

Just like Nicole, many of us have a tendency to want to approve God's plan before we start working it. We get one instruction, and we find ourselves asking God why that doesn't make any sense? Wouldn't it just be easier if you did it this way? Because we have our walls up, we typically cannot trust anyone to get things done. Every time we trust someone with something that is important, we are often let down and disappointed. All of this affects our ability to relinquish control. It's our way of protecting and guarding ourselves. I can absolutely relate to Nicole. I'm the dependable sister, daughter, friend, and coworker. As you read through this devotional today, are you able to pinpoint parts of yourself in Nicole's story? If this is you, what the Lord is saying is, "You don't need to have those walls up with me. You can trust me to get it done. You don't need to be strong with me. Just lean into my strength. You can depend on me," says God. "I only plan good things for you. You don't need to know the plan. You just need to know the God who created the plan." What I love the most about what the Lord is saying here is that he just wants us to rest in the identity of being his daughter. You are a daughter of God and when you truly begin to rest in that identity, you'll realize you don't need to be in control anymore, worrying if things are going to work out. Because you know your father has everything in control and all his ways are perfect, and his Word is flawless, he Shields all those who take refuge in him (Psalms 18:30).

Take a moment to pray this prayer:

Father God, I ask you to forgive me for not trusting in your plan by faith. Help me, Father, to submit my earthly wisdom to your sovereign wisdom. I've relinquished control and I forgive everyone in the past that has ever let me down. Because I know if I trust you wholeheartedly, you never will. No longer will I allow my earthly relationships to affect my relationship with you. Please, Lord, continue to reveal to me the things that are preventing me from trusting you and inheriting your promises to me. You are a holy God who cannot lie, and for this reason, I will trust you. In Jesus name, amen!

Day 12
The Multidimensional God

"In the fourth generation your descendants will come back here, for the sin of the Amorites has not yet reached its full measure."
Genesis 15:16 NIV

One thing I had to learn quickly in my silent seasons was, If I did everything I was supposed to do as instructed by the Lord and he is silent, I had to recognize that it wasn't my move and it was God's turn. In the silent seasons, I quickly realized that God is a multidimensional God. Meaning that he wasn't just concerned about me and what I wanted, but he was also concerned about everyone involved. With this knowledge, once I did everything I was supposed to do on my end, and it was God's turn, I would begin to start praying for everyone else involved. For example, a friend of mine was trying to buy a house. The Lord had instructed her to start looking, but after a couple of months of not finding what she wanted, she started to get frustrated with the process. I spoke to her and quickly shifted her perspective. I said God is not only concerned about you. There is someone sitting in the house he has for you, struggling with the idea of selling it. He also needs to make sure that when they leave the house, they are going to be OK in their new place and that they have what they need as well. You're only worried about you, while God is worried about everyone involved. You are his daughter, but that person is also his son or daughter. I instructed her to start praying for everyone involved. She started praying that the current owner of the house would come into alignment with the will of God for their lives and that they would have peace to sell. She quickly changed her perspective and began to pray accordingly and now she is the owner of the house that met all her desires. In this passage of scripture, God is revealing the reason to Abraham as to why his descendants will not inherit the Promise land right away. It was already occupied by the Amorites, and it was not yet justifiable to move them from the land and give it to the children of Israel.

We have a tendency to be so narrow-minded in the place of prayer, praying for ourselves and those that we know praying for a promotion on our job, not realizing that the person currently sitting in our seat of promotion has been going back and forth in their minds to apply for a new job. We need to pray that they would be courageous that the fear of change will not stop them from stepping into what God wants for them so we can step into what God has for us.

Think for a moment what you have been praying for? Have you been praying for everyone involved? Have you been praying good things for them as well? Pray for the person occupying the land you want and know that God is always working behind the scenes. So, when you don't see him working in your life, know that it's because he's working in the life of the person connected to the situation. Even if you don't know them, he is a multidimensional God.

Repent for being impatient and not understanding that God is always working. Agree with Heaven that you will change your prayer strategy.

Make a list of your prayer requests. What could the people on the other end of your request be struggling with, preventing them from making the decision that will benefit you both?

Day 13
The Power of Perspective

"And we know that God causes everything to work together for the good of those who love God, and are called according to his purpose for them."
Romans 8:28

This is one of my favorite scriptures to focus on when I make a bad decision and unknowingly step outside of the will of God. That God, in his sovereignty, will use the situation, experience, and circumstance to make sure it's not completely wasted, but that something good will come out of it. I remember dating someone I thought would be the one, only to find myself drifting further and further away from God. I barely made it out of that relationship with my soul and salvation intact. But glory to God for pulling me out. Once I was out and after repenting for being out of God's will, this scripture was laid on my heart, and I prayed earnestly to ask God to reveal to me the good in that very horrible season. And he did! God used that man to reveal parts of myself that still needed to be worked on. I went into that season strong, got weak and came out 10 times stronger. Could I have achieved personal development and growth under better circumstances? Absolutely, but God played with the cards I dealt him. When God is playing their hand, no hand is a bad hand because he's so strategic he's going to win anyways.

I share this story because sometimes we have a tendency not to step out on faith because we are afraid that we might make a mistake and mess things up, that we might make the wrong decision. But if we would really grab a hold of Romans 8:28, we would know that God and his sovereignty has a way of making your biggest mess ups bless you in the biggest ways. It was in that relationship where my perspective on money and investments shifted, which caused me to make decisions concerning my house that is bringing in an extra $1000 per month.

Have you ever looked at a season in your life where you said nothing good came out of it. Maybe you're so disappointed with that season that fear has set in concerning that area of your life. I want to challenge you to look again because something in that season worked for your good. The storms don't come to destroy you. They prepare you to carry the weight of your destiny. Yes! Even the self-inflicted storms, thanks to God, have a way of preparing you for your destiny. No weapon formed against you will prosper Isaiah 54:17, But it will all work together for your good.

Recall your most difficult season and pray and ask God to show you the good that came out of it. Write down what is revealed here. When you change your perspective on your most difficult seasons, you come to appreciate what God did through it, eliminating room for fears and doubts to take up residence.

Day 14
The Power of Purpose

"Moses said to the Lord, "Pardon your servant, Lord. I have never been eloquent, neither in the past nor since you have spoken to your servant. I am slow of speech and tongue. The Lord said to him, "Who gave human beings their mouths? Who makes them deaf or mute? Who gives them sight or makes them blind? Is it not I, the Lord? Now go; I will help you speak and will teach you what to say."
Exodus 4:10-12

Moses was educated in all the wisdom of the Egyptians and was powerful in speech and action.
Act 7:22

I remember when the Lord first told me what my purpose was, I responded by saying OK. I was happy to finally know what I needed to do to bring me to the place that the Lord had shown me many years earlier. Except, less than two weeks later, when I truly realized what the Lord wanted me to do, I stood in my kitchen and said God, I can't do that. I've never done anything like that before. I'm a nurse, that's not my area of expertise. The Lord responded by saying Dennisha, what do you think you've been doing for the past two years with your friends? I said God, is that what I was doing? I thought I was just being a good friend? Since stepping out in faith, I have discovered so much untapped potential, things

I didn't even know I was capable of. Gifts I didn't even know I had, like personality traits that set me apart from everyone else and strategically aid in the fulfillment of my purpose. Quirks that some people don't like that's built into me for my specific purpose. My purpose has produced potential, and I realized that I was "built like this" so that I could be "built for this." As a result of that revelation, I stopped taking what was different about me for granted and started embracing it.

We have a tendency to doubt our capabilities when we are asked to do something that is unfamiliar. Unable to realize that God is the very one who formed us in our mother's womb and when he formed us, he knew exactly what he wanted us to be able to do when we got here. With that knowledge, he made sure everything we needed to accomplish the purpose he created us for was built into us at that time. We are filled with untapped potential for a purpose. When we start to do anything that is connected to that purpose, we will begin to unveil parts of ourselves that we didn't even know were there.

How many times have you refused to do something because you believed you were not able to do it? How many divine opportunities have you missed because you counted yourself out? How much-buried potential is crying out on the inside of you, waiting to fulfill its purpose? How many people have made you feel insecure about a part of you that God is saying I made you that way on purpose? How many people have told you to be quiet or you talk too much when God is saying I created you to be a world-renowned speaker? But because of past criticism, you're afraid to speak in front of crowds. There's a beautiful unveiling of yourself that will happen when you step out into your purpose, into the unknown.

What is it that God has been asking you to do, but your insecurities have allowed fear to stop you from discovering your true potential?

Write it down here. Pray and get fresh instructions, then step out on faith and watch yourself bloom! Whatever it is God is asking you to do in this season, you're built for it!

Day 15
The Power of Application

"For the Word of God is living and active and full of power [making it operative, energizing, and effective]. It is sharper than any two-edged [b] sword, penetrating as far as the division of the [c]soul and spirit [the completeness of a person], and of both joints and marrow [the deepest parts of our nature], exposing and judging the very thoughts and intentions of the heart."
Hebrews 4:12 AMP

The moment I realized that the application of God's Word brought transformation to my life, I would constantly ask God to reveal the parts of me that was displeasing to Him. I wanted Him to highlight something about me that was not of him so I could deal with it. I would begin to search the Word of God to start removing that thing, meditating on the scriptures that relate to it, and apply those scriptures to my life. Before I knew it, I was a completely different person. The things that used to bother me before didn't bother me anymore. I was immensely filled with the peace of God and my level of faith was out of this world. All my insecurities melted away, along with fear and doubt. Eventually, I reached the happiest I've ever been in my entire life, and it had nothing to do with external things. It was literally the internal work that was done through the application of God's Word that brought healing to my soul. I no longer feel broken and discarded, but I feel whole and filled with power.

We have a tendency to read the Bible just for reading sake or just for encouragement to see if God would speak to our situation through his Word. But the biggest injustice we do ourselves and the Word of God is not applying it. If the Word of God is sharper than every double-edged sword and it created the heavens and the earth, how much more will it be able to do in our lives if we diligently apply it?

Have you ever intentionally applied a portion of scripture to your life for an extended period while making a conscious effort daily to carry it out? The Word of the Lord tells us that God's Word will not return to him void. So, when you apply it, you must see the fruit of that application. When you consistently resist the enemy when he comes to try and steal that fruit, he will flee, and you will end up with fruit that will remain. One of the main reasons we don't step out on faith to do what God is instructing us is because we are afraid we won't see fruit. But when we lack patience and we begin to do what the Word says regarding patience, we will start to see the fruit of the Word develop in our lives. As a result, nothing will hold us back from stepping out in faith.

Think of 1 character flaw you want to improve, then search the Word of God for scriptures related to it. Write them down, meditate on them daily, and make the conscious decision every day to come into alignment with it, casting down every thought that is contrary to it. Do this every day and watch how you begin to transform.

46

Day 16
The Power of Biblical Meditation

"This Book of the Law shall not depart from your mouth, but you shall read [and meditate on] it day and night, so that you may be careful to do [everything] in accordance with all that is written in it; for then you will make your way prosperous, and then you will be [d]successful."
Joshua 1:8 AMP

One of the biggest oppositions to our spiritual growth as believers is spiritual warfare. The number one attack the enemy uses to attack us is by attacking our minds. Throughout my spiritual growth journey, I realized the benefits of meditating on God's Word. I would have a scripture for every situation. When a situation would arise and my response, whether physically or emotionally, was not in alignment with God's word/will for my life, I would repeat that scripture repeatedly. For example, whenever I was trying to walk by faith and not by sight and doubt would creep in, I would start meditating on Jeremiah 29:11. I would recite repeatedly I know the plans God has towards me, plans of good and not evil. I would repeatedly meditate on it, and as a result, my mind was renewed. This strategy would expose the lies and negative thoughts in my mind because the truth of God's Word was revealed. By doing this, I would cast down every vain imagination and I would not submit to the lies, doubt, or fear, but I would then come into alignment with God's Word. Because I meditated on God's Word concerning every area of my life, not only am I prospering spiritually, but I'm also prospering physically, mentally, and emotionally. My soul has prospered because I meditate on the Word of God. When I was still struggling with insecurities, I would meditate on Psalms 139:14. I am fearfully and wonderfully made.

Our life is a product of our thoughts. (As a man thinketh, so is he. Proverbs 23:7) if we are meditating on lies, then we cannot expect the results to be what God has declared. In order to receive the result of God's Word (truth), we have to meditate on the truth (God's Word). Meditating on God's Word has the power to renew our minds, reveal truth, and cast out vain imaginations.

What areas of your life are you constantly battling thoughts that you know is not your heavenly father's will for your life? What are you struggling with today? Is it fear, doubt, loneliness, depression? Whatever you're struggling with today, there are plenty of scriptures that relate to it. Write them down, meditate on them day and night, and watch how you begin to prosper in those areas. God's Word does not return to him void (without fruit), so it will produce fruit in your life. Believe it.

Day 17
God's Motivation

"Then God said, "Let us make mankind in our image, in our likeness, so that they may rule over the fish in the sea and the birds in the sky, over the livestock and all the wild animals,[a] and over all the creatures that move along the ground"
Genesis 1:26 NIV

Years ago, when I first surrendered my life to Christ and discovered this passage of scripture, I wept. Because I realized that society and myself included, had drifted so far from the image of God that when we look into the mirror, we don't look anything like him. All I could imagine was blurred pixels where you are unable to make out the image. From that day on, I was determined to become the image of God that he intended me to reflect from the very beginning of time. I dived into his Word & prayer and allowed him to peel back the layers of me that did not reflect him. The more of the process I allowed God to take me through, the more he would reveal himself to me. As a result, I fell deep in love with God. He gave me an understanding of who he is, how he works, and why he does what he does. This knowledge has provided me with revelation of how to team up with God to accomplish his purpose in my life and on this earth. Knowing all that I know about God, I'm not afraid that I won't be happy with his choice for me. Because the innermost woven parts of my being, whether I know it or not, is crying out for it.

God's greatest motivation is to transform us back into his image so that we would have dominion. When we live our life, read the Word, and filter scripture through this knowledge, it allows us to become the best version of ourselves. The only version that is God-approved, the version that is full of faith and has no Fear. The version that has dominion over every life circumstance. The version that impacts the lives and communities around us. The version that draws other people with the love and character of God to Christ. The version that completely embodies what it means to be one with God (John 14) abide in me and I will abide in you). The version where no matter where you are, you feel like you're in Eden. "Become the best version of yourself" is such a common phrase used today. However, I'll tell you this one truth, unless the best version of yourself is the version that God approves of and is destined for, in Genesis 1:26, then it's really not the best version of yourself. You'll always find yourself lacking and wanting more, not quite able to figure out exactly what is missing. Your inner man is crying out to be what it was created to be, in the image and likeness of God so it can have dominion over fear, depression, misery, hurt, pain, poverty, sickness, death, etc. Jesus came that we would have life and have it more abundantly, and he left the Holy Spirit behind to help us, to teach us, and guide us, on how to reach that place of abundance and eternal life.

Pray this prayer: Father God, I realize that I'm not who you intended me to be when you created man. Lord, I confess now that my desire is to look like you, walk like you, talk like you, and function like you. That I will be one with you and fulfill my purpose here on earth. God, I acknowledge that I cannot fulfill my purpose with a version of myself that is not fit to fulfill it. Help me to become the version of me that is needed to fulfill the purpose that is locked up on the inside of me! In Jesus name I pray, Amen.

Day 18
Navigating The Seasons (Identification)

"Search me, God, and know my heart; test me and know my anxious thoughts.
See if there is any offensive way in me, and lead me in the way everlasting."
Psalms 139:23-24 NIV

In an effort to become the reflective image of God, I often find myself doing inventory checks, taking the time and initiative to ask God to reveal to me something he sees in me that is not in alignment with his will or desire for me. But then there was this one time where I didn't ask, and God just came right out and told me. I still remember how broken I felt because I couldn't understand how I had even gotten to this place. It was one of those days where I just didn't feel like getting out of bed and the Lord said to me Dennisha, you have to take better care of yourself because if you don't, when the promise I have made you comes to fruition you won't be able to maintain it or sustain it. As I meditated on what the Lord was saying, I realized I had put myself on the back burner of my own life. I would spend all my time and energy making sure that everyone else was OK. Making sure that everyone else was satisfied, that I neglected myself, my needs, my health, my wants, my desires, and what made me feel like my best. Whenever it came to myself, I would often say I'll eat later. I can wait. I can do without. I'm too tired to do this for me but always find the energy to do it for someone else. That day I cried uncontrollably. I went on a journey to the past to figure out how I got here. I wasn't always like this. Only to discover that the root of my self-neglect was parenthood.

As women, we are created to be nurturers, so if we are not careful, we find ourselves nurturing, cultivating, and building up our loved ones while neglecting ourselves. Wanting so much for our children, spouses, and loved ones that we forget about all the things we need.

On the list of all your priorities, where do you fall? How important is your growth, self-development, dreams, mental health, healing? The one thing you need to learn about the difficult seasons of your life is that they are difficult because it highlights something in your character that needs developing. The more you focus on how hard the season is you're going to miss the part of you that God is trying to improve and fine-tune. You are a priority, just as much as your loved ones are a priority. Find harmony and let God build you the same way he's using you to build others.

Pray this prayer: Father, if there are any areas of my life that I have been neglecting and overlooking, please forgive me and reveal it to me. My desire is to be successful and fruitful in all areas of my life. I surrender to your cultivating process in every season of my life. Please take control, that I will find harmony and balance in allowing you to develop me as you use me to develop others.

Day 19
Navigating The Seasons (Cultivation)

"Every good and perfect gift is from above, coming down from the Father of the heavenly lights, who does not change like shifting shadows."
James 1:7 NIV

I remember going through a very difficult season in my single-ness. I fell to my knees and cried out in prayer. I said Lord, I desire to be married again someday but don't send him until I'm ready because I don't want to ruin a good thing. Sometimes we are so familiar with ourselves that we can be quick to say to someone, "Well, this is how I am," or "I've always been this way." During that season, I had to realize that even though I have always been considered a good person there were still some things in my character that needed improvement and just because I've always been this way doesn't mean I have to stay this way. I became de-termined to become the gift that my Father in heaven would give to whomever my Kingdom spouse was going to be. If all good gifts came from God, and I wanted him to present me to my Kingdom spouse, I had to make sure that I became a good gift, an answered prayer. I realized that the same way I'm praying for my husband to have certain qualities and characteristics, he's also praying the same thing. If I did not allow God to groom and cultivate those qualities in me, then he would not recognize me as the answer to his prayers when he met me.

We have a tendency to require something from others that we ourselves don't possess. We must come to the realization that God will not give us something, only to turn around and watch us ruin it or become ruined by it. In order to inherit the promises of God, we have to make sure that we are ready spiritually and physically. Spiritually so that God doesn't lose us to the promise. Physically, so that we don't lose the promise because we are physically unable to maintain and sustain it.

You must realize that because God is a jealous God, and his gifts maketh rich and add no sorrow (Proverbs 10:22), God cannot, according to his holy character, give you something that is going to add sorrow to your life because you don't have the necessary character to maintain it. God is a God of covenant, keeping his promises for generations, but he will not compete with his own promise for your love and attention. As you think about the petitions you have before the Lord, ask yourself this question. Am I physically and spiritually equipped to receive what it is I'm waiting for right now?

For the last 19 days, we have touched on the idea of cultivation repeatedly. Take a moment today and sit with the Holy Spirit and write down all the reasons why it's so important. Brainstorm the things that will never change if you never change.

Day 20

Navigating The Seasons (Harvests)

When someone has been given much, much will be required in return; and when someone has been entrusted with much, even more will be required.
Luke 12:48 NLT

When I finally discovered that many seasons of trials was simply God trying to determine if he can get out of me what he has been trying to cultivate in me, my life changed. And so did my perspective on the sovereignty of God. He would use situations to determine if I was ready. Would she be patient, would she give out of her need, would she value knowing where her next check was coming from over what I have said? And every time, I would pass the test. Why did I pass the test? Because I knew it was a test, and all of God's tests are open books. When you expect to be tested, you're always ready for the test. But here's another problem I discovered. When the enemy knows that God is testing you, he will come in and tempt you because he does not want you to pass the test. Here's the difference. The temptation is going to be pleasing to the flesh. We know the flesh is always at enmity with God, which can make it harder to pass the test if you can't put your flesh under subjection.

We have a tendency to fail the test repeatedly, not because the test was so hard but because the temptation was so good. We begin to justify our reasons for choosing the wrong action. This is where I will always say we can't allow our emotions to dictate our actions.

As you continue to allow God to cultivate in you what he wants to get out of you, be prepared for the test that will most definitely come as a result of the cultivation process. I call it the olive press. When you are harvesting olive oil from olives, the olive has to go through the press three times. Just like Jesus in the Garden of Gethsemane and in the wilderness, don't just pass the first test and fail the others. Be sure to pass them all. It's easier to pass a test that you know is coming because you are prepared for it. When you pass the testing, you enter into a season of receiving.

Consider what you are cultivating in this season and what kind of things can you start doing now to prepare your spirit man to pass the test, so you don't fulfill the lust of the flesh?

Day 21
Navigating The Seasons (Reaping & Receiving)

"So let's not get tired of doing what is good. At just the right time we will reap a harvest of blessing if we don't give up."
Galatians 6:9 NLT

I have friends who are big visionaries. They have tons of dreams and visions related to what God has promised them. Because they have so much vision when God first shows them anything and tells them what to do, they are initially super excited about the idea and begin to run full speed ahead. But as they run into problems along the way, they begin to lose sight of the possibility of their vision coming to pass. When I think of them, I think of the melodic phrase, "Can we skip to the good part?"

And let's be honest, whether we are big visionaries or not, we all wish we could skip straight to the reaping and receiving stage, where we receive the promise. But it is truly in our best interest to go through the process and not just go through it but to be able to identify the process along the way. Why? Because we are called to be testimonies of Christ and to disciple others. If we want to disciple others, we need to be able to identify the process so that we can replicate the results. You cannot teach what you do not know and what you have not identified. If your business makes $1,000,000, but you don't clearly identify what worked and what doesn't, you won't be able to replicate it or teach your grandchildren how to do it so that you can produce generational wealth.

Have you ever been stuck and had to figure out something on your own, and by the time you finally figure it out, you have no idea how you got there? You just stumbled across this solution, and you don't even know what you did. This happens to me sometimes with computer issues. Don't ask me how I fixed it, but it's fixed. If you can't teach someone how to do something, then you really don't know how to do it. This is why when wealthy people lose all their money, they can start all over and build it all again. But people who win the lottery often go broke in a few years because they haven't gone through the process of learning how to obtain, sustain, and maintain it. One of my biggest pet peeves in the body of Christ is everyone telling you to have faith, but nobody tells you how. By the grace of God and the building of my own faith, I have identified the process of teaching others how to enter into new dimensions of faith. The Word of God didn't tell us to just be fruitful, it told us to be fruitful and multiply. You cannot multiply what you cannot replicate. If you tell someone how to do something and they apply it, but it doesn't bring forth fruit for them, then you haven't learned how to multiply it.

Pray this prayer: Father, help me not to be frustrated with the process. But help me to identify how you're getting me to my destination so that I will be a good disciple and be able to strengthen my brothers and sisters in Christ. That I would be able to teach others how to do the same. Help me to not get so distracted by the journey that I don't recognize which keys have opened which doors along the way. In Jesus name I pray, Amen.

Day 22
Season of Separation

"The Lord had said to Abram, "Leave your native country, your relatives, and your father's family, and go to the land that I will show you. **²** *I will make you into a great nation. I will bless you and make you famous, and you will be a blessing to others.* **³** *I will bless those who bless you and curse those who treat you with contempt. All the families on earth will be blessed through you."*
Genesis 12:1-2 NLT

The season of separation was one of the hardest seasons the Lord took me through to build my faith. In this season, there was a drastic change in my relationships. I felt alone, misunderstood, abandoned, and neglected. My loved ones became distant and changed the way they interacted with me. And to be honest, I didn't do anything wrong. We didn't have any kind of falling out, things just changed. As I prayed to God about what was going on in my relationships, he responded by saying Dennisha, I am separating you to elevate you. It was a nice idea. I mean, God, it sounds good, but it didn't feel good, not one bit! I thought to myself how I was going to get through this season and appreciate what God was doing because all I felt was hurt and pain? I knew it wasn't personal, but it sure felt personal.

We have a tendency to take the season of separation personally. It was through that season that the Lord revealed to me that if we have an issue with abandonment, neglect, and insecurities from our past, we tend to take this season personally. If we find ourselves taking it personally, we have to seek the Lord to find out what it is he is working out of us in that season so that he can elevate us. This season teaches us how to lean on God and stay the course even when everyone else says otherwise.

In order for certain plants to grow well, it needs to be planted a certain amount of feet away from other plants. If it isn't planted a specific amount of feet away from other plants, it will begin to grow a fungus on its leaves because it is suffocating. At this point, the plant is now contaminated and puts the other plants around it at risk of being contaminated as well. In this season, God has to separate you in order to elevate you because he does not want you to be contaminated. He wants you to get into his presence and flourish. You need the space to grow. Please understand that this is only for a season. Just because you're going to do well alone in this season doesn't mean you're going to stay alone. Don't be discouraged but embrace what God is doing in the season of separation. Because as you grow and God waters you, nothing will contaminate you and you will flourish. When you come out of the season of separation, everyone will see the growth. They will notice the glow because you have been in the presence of the Lord. You're being separated to be elevated.

Pray this prayer: Father God help me to be at peace with the season of separation that I won't despise it, but I will embrace it. Help me to deal with all the root issues that you reveal to me that causes me to take the season of separation personally. Father, I am ready for elevation in my life, so help me to navigate the season of separation well. In Jesus name I pray, Amen.

Day 23
Stages of Prophetic Fulfillment

"Until the time that his Word [of prophecy regarding his brothers] came true,
The Word of the Lord tested and refined him."
Psalm 105:19 AMP

One thing I realized is that the prophetic Word of God comes to prove you, test you, and refine you. It's not just about receiving the promise, it's about the process God takes me through to build my capacity to receive the promise. When I look at the life of Joseph in the Bible, I can see how God's promise proved him in the pit, tested him in the palace, and refined him in prison. All before the dream that the Lord revealed to him came to pass. I don't always like the way God chooses to equip me for the promise, but I always love and appreciate the results.

We have a tendency to lose faith in the process because it seems contrary to the promise. But the process is needed for God to PROVE that we love and trust him even when our lives start to go in the opposite direction than what he promised us. It's the same way God proved Abraham's faith during the years Sarah couldn't conceive, even though God told Abraham that Sarah would bring forth a son. The process is needed to TEST us in our place of increase to make sure we will continue to serve God in the high place and not value the promise above honoring God. Just like when Joseph was tested in the palace with Potiphar's wife. Joseph continued to refuse her repeatedly, choosing to Honor God above his position. The process is needed to REFINE our character when we've lost everything. Just like God refined Job's character by removing all remnants of pride and self-righteousness. Just like he refined the children of Israel in the wilderness. To receive the promise, you have to be willing to go through the process of being proved, tested, and refined. Will you trust God when you have nothing? Will you honor God when you have everything? And can you still trust God when you lose it all? If you can't pass all three of those tests, God will continue to process you, until you do. It's important to be processed for the promise, your soul depends on it. Joseph was proven in the pit, tested in the palace, and refined in the prison before he was appointed 2nd in command to the pharaoh.

Identify what stage of prophetic fulfillment you're in. Are you in the first stage, the proving stage, where your life starts going in the opposite direction of what God just promised you. The second stage is where your life begins to receive an increase that looks like the coming promise, but your decision to honor God will cause you to lose it all. Or are you in the third stage where you are in the wilderness, you have given up your comforts for God and you are unable to lay hold of the promise and you feel like you're back to square one? The truth is you're not at square one. You are literally standing at the edge of the promise land, thinking that you will never crossover. Don't make the wrong decisions in the third stage.

Pray this prayer: Father God please help me to identify the seasons you have me in. Continue to prepare my heart to be proved, tested, and refined for your glory. I do not want to lose you because of the promise. I also don't want to lose the promise because I'm not ready for it. Father, I welcome the seasons of prophetic fulfillment and I ask for your help to navigate them well. In Jesus name I pray, Amen.

Day 24
Power of Communication

"Man's steps are ordered and ordained by the LORD. How then can a man [fully] understand his way?"
Proverbs 20:24 AMP

I remember walking in a Plaza parking lot with a friend of mine and as we walked and talked about God, I got a flashback vision of many pass encounters where she and I were praying together. Then the Lord said to me she will pray earnestly for an extended period of time, 30 minutes, 40 minutes easy. But then, once she is done praying (talking) to me, she immediately gets up and goes on about making herself busy. The Lord said she never sits still & quiet long enough in my presence after she's done praying to allow me a chance to respond. The Lord then showed me a vision of a husband and wife having a conversation where the husband talked and talked and talked, expressing his feelings and voicing his argument. Then when he was done talking, he turned around and walked away. The Lord asked me how do you think that made the wife feel. She never got the opportunity to respond?

We have a tendency to treat God this way when we pray, complain, and make our request known, followed by an Amen and walking away, never being quiet long enough to listen to his response. We can't follow the instructions of the Lord pertaining to our prayers if we don't sit long enough to obtain the instruction.

Why do we do this? I truly believe that the reason why we find ourselves doing this is because we can't physically see God in front of us while we are praying. We know it's rude and disrespectful to walk away from someone who is trying to talk to us. So why do we do it to God? If God is the one that orders our steps, then we need to listen for the orders. Some things we pray for are granted immediately and do not require you to do anything. But other things we pray for require us to obey a set of instructions. We miss a lot of instructions when we pray on the go.

Can you recall the last time where you sat still after prayer just to listen and ask God to speak to you? Without telling God what answer you wanted him to give you. It's easier to hear God speak in silence when you have an open heart to receive anything he has to say, even when it might not be what you want to hear. It is not God's desire for us to walk around in ignorance to everything. Remember, you can only team up with God when you know what he wants to do. In order for you to walk into everything God has for you, you have to diligently seek him for instructions and listen for his response.

Take a moment to write out a simple prayer concerning one thing from one area of your life. Tell God what you want but let him know wholeheartedly that you will surrender your desire to his will (which is perfect for you). Then ask the Lord to instruct you so you can come into alignment with his will. Then, take a moment to sit quietly with no distractions for 10 minutes and genuinely give the Lord an opportunity to respond right away. You have to trust that he will find a way to get his instructions to you, even if it's not at that moment.

Day 25
Overcoming Fear

"For God did not give us a spirit of timidity or cowardice or fear, but [He has given us a spirit] of power and of love and of sound judgment and personal discipline [abilities that result in a calm, well-balanced mind and self-control]."
2 Timothy 1:7 AMP

"But when he, the Spirit of truth, comes, he will guide you into all the truth. He will not speak on his own; he will speak only what he hears, and he will tell you what is yet to come."
John 16:13 NIV

I distinctly remember an 18-hour encounter with the spirit of fear. It left me feeling crippled and it was very difficult to breathe. I had this heaviness on my chest that just would not go away. I would try and avoid how I was feeling by engaging in conversation with others, but it was very difficult because the thoughts associated with the fear were nonstop. Before I knew it, brief thoughts of suicide were creeping in. I was aggravated and irritated and I didn't want to talk to anyone. I wanted silence, but I also feared the silence. Why? Because I was now left alone with my own thoughts. I was unable to focus and couldn't think straight. During conversations, I would only hear 50% of what the other person was saying. I was exhausted, dealing with the spirit of fear, was taking me out. It resurfaced my past, attacked my present, and tried to rob me of my hope for the future. I realized that there were several things reinforcing the fear, but the number one thing was doubt.

I learned in that 18-hour period of crippling fear that if we want to overcome fear, we have to eliminate doubt. Once we understand that doubt is an open door that allows fear to come in, we can better guard our hearts against the spirit of fear, worry, and anxiety.

Doubt is the culprit. If you get rid of the doubt then the spirit of fear will have no legal rights to attack you. God did not give you a spirit of fear. He gave you his spirit, the spirit of truth, a spirit of power, love, and a sound mind.

Take a moment to identify all the things you're afraid of, then brainstorm all the doubts you have concerning that area of your life.

Pray this prayer:

Father God, I acknowledge that you have not given me a spirit of fear but a spirit of power, love, and sound mind. Lord, on this day, I choose to relinquish all my fears to you. I trust that your ways are perfect concerning me. I will not be afraid of the future because I know my future is in your hands. In Jesus name I pray, Amen.

Day 26
Overcoming Doubt

"Immediately the boy's father exclaimed, "I do believe; help me overcome my unbelief!"
Mark 9:24 NIV

And we know that in all things God works for the good of those who love him, who[i] have been called according to his purpose.
Romans 8:28 NIV

I'm always determined to find Romans 8:28 (God makes all things work together for your good) in every season of my life, whether the seasons are good, bad, or indifferent. Whether they are short-lived or long-lasting, I try my best to step back and get a divine perspective. Because if I can find the good to focus on, then the bad won't be so bad because it's all working out in the end. Because I have a natural gift to identify strategy, after that 18hr encounter with fear, doubt, and anxiety, I came out of that season with knowledge of the enemy's strategy and how to counteract it. We learned yesterday that the enemy uses doubt to reinforce fear. During those 18hrs, every time I would put my focus on something that strengthens the doubt (Googling worst case scenario), the fear would become increasingly reinforced. I learned that doubt also works by going back into your past, reminding you of past events and connecting dots as to why you should doubt the truth. Doubt is an information gatherer. Doubt collects false evidence and makes it appear real (F.E.A.R = False evidence appearing real). The serpent beguiled Eve by letting her doubt the truth of what God said by giving her false information (lie). The one thing I had to do to stop experiencing high levels of fear was to stop Googling what I was so afraid of. Because when I did, doubt kicked into full gear and went to work, connecting all sorts of dots that I started considering as solid evidence.

Even in fearful situations, we have to be able to take a moment and analyze what is making this worse. What is making us increasingly doubtful? The only way we can remove doubt as a reinforcer is by combating it with the truth. The more time we spend reading the truth of God's Word and seeking God's perspective concerning the situation by asking him to show us the good in it, only then will we be able to hold on to the truth and let go of the doubt. There is something in every season that God wants us to learn that is divinely connected to our purpose. Why? Because God has the sovereign ability to conform the enemy's plans to work together with his plan for our future. We can't focus on what the enemy is doing because we'll only strengthen his plans. But if we shift our focus to what God is trying to do in that season, then we'll be able to appreciate it on a whole new level.

In order for you to overcome doubt, you have to feed your spirit with truth, repent of doubting, and command the spirit of fear to go. It's the lies of the enemy that is causing you to doubt what God said and as a result, you're too afraid to step out on faith. Maybe you step out on faith, but you retreat when things are not working out, or you start taking matters into your own hands, doing things in a way that you think will work better. All because the fear that it won't work out God's way is too much for you not to intervene with your human wisdom. Can you recall a time where the more doubtful you became, the more fearful you became? Now that you are out of that season and you have a clearer mind, analyze it! What were the things that caused your doubt to increase? How did your level of fear and anxiety respond to the increased doubt? As you analyze that season earnestly, pray that God will reveal to you what was the good he wanted you to get out of that season.

Day 27
Overcoming Worry

"Worry weighs a person down;
an encouraging word cheers a person up.
Proverbs 12:25 NLT

Call me weird, but I enjoy uncovering the tactics of the enemy and I know that is a very strange way to start a devotional on worry. But hopefully, by day 27, you've realized this is not your average devotional. I don't know about anyone else, but I don't want to just have God moments. I need everlasting solution. With that being said, let's continue this discussion on my 18 hours of intense warfare on my mind. While doubt dug up my past, highlighted my present, and tapped into my future worry was a full-blown attack on my future, my hopes, and my dreams. I worried so much that it all started to crumble before my eyes. The vision God gave me took a complete shift as I worried about how my present circumstance was going to impact my future security, safety, health, family, career. I was on the front line of battle in my own mind, and it seemed like I was losing. I quickly realized I needed another external voice because the thoughts that were running through my mind had me contemplating suicide. I was losing hope in everything I dreamed of, so what was the point of living? Thankfully a friend called me just when I was about to break down crying again, and instead of being the strong private person I always am, I simply told her the truth, I am not OK. She was my voice of reason for the entire 18 hours. Even though it was difficult to believe in her optimism, talking to her saved me from dwelling on my own negative thoughts.

We have a tendency to not seek out help when we need it the most. We don't want anyone to see our weaknesses. We don't want anyone to get tired of us. We don't want anyone to judge us wrongfully, and that's all understandable. But it's imperative that we have covenant friends that we can trust and confide in. Friends that have a relationship with the Holy Spirit & can obey the nudging to call us when we need it the most. But when they call, it's on us to speak up and admit we are in a bad place. Worrying can cause us to make bad decisions that will end up pushing us backward and not forward.

You can't keep making wrong decisions and still expect to end up at your divine destination on time. Faith in God as your loving father has the ability to eliminate all your worries. The question is, do you view God as a loving father? Can you, in the midst of your worries, remember back to a time when God was loving and faithful in a difficult season? Can you find comfort like I did in the scriptures he's given you in the past? Remembering the faithfulness of God and having friends that can remind you of his faithfulness can melt all your worries away.

Pray this prayer: Father God, I ask that you strengthen my covenant relationships or send me a covenant friend whom I can trust and confide in. Help us to build our relationship on the strength and truth of your Word that we would be destiny helpers to each other. Please protect our relationship from the devices of the enemy and help us to always be loving and honest with each other. Give us wisdom and insight so that we would be able to uplift each other at the right time. In Jesus name I pray, Amen.

Day 28
Overcoming Anxiety

"Cast all your anxiety on him because he cares for you.
1 Peter 5:7 NIV

In those 18 hours, I quickly realized that worry truly is the root of anxiety. When my anxiety reached its threshold, it left this heaviness on my chest that made it seem very difficult to breathe. I could not catch my own breath. The heaviness was constantly there, reminding me that I'm afraid of something. Reminding me that I'm filled with doubt, reminding me that my life is being hijacked. No matter how hard I would try to forget my worries, the elephant sitting on my chest wouldn't allow me to forget. The anxiety I had over the health scare I was experiencing was unreal. Even after revelation and truth came in and after the fear was gone, the heaviness on my chest was still lingering around. I was no longer fearful. I now knew what God was doing, and even though I didn't like the way he chose to do it, I was completely appreciative of the why. The why was so big, the why brought clarity, the why was a key to success in life. But the way made me unable to fully exhale. In those 18 hours, anxiety was the last battle I had to fight. It was trying to hold on to the end.

We tend to equate anxiety with troubles. But we must realize that anxiety has a tendency to remain behind even after the troubles are no longer seen as a threat. Keeping that awkward heaviness on your chest and knot in the pit of your stomach. At this point, we must acknowledge that the anxiousness is now an illegal invader. And there's a war going on in your members.

Prayer and true worship have the wonderful ability to take you from an anxious state to a peaceful state of mind. Because God inhabits the praises of his people, when you praise God whole-heartedly, you welcome his presence and invoke his spirit. Unexplainable peace comes from God, so even when society thinks you shouldn't be at peace, you will be.

Pray and invite the peace of God to come in and melt your anxiety away. Exhale all the anxiety and worries and inhale the peace of God.

Father God, I repent for worrying and feeling anxious about my current situation. I trust that my life is in your hands and that your plans for me are good and not evil. I come into agreement with your Word that anyone whose heart and mind is stayed on you that you would bring them into perfect peace. Father, I asked that you would, by the power of repentance, destroy the legal right for the spirit of anxiety to function in my life, and I cast it out of my atmosphere now in the name of Jesus. May the spirit of peace rest, rule, and abide in me and in my atmosphere. In Jesus name I pray, Amen.

Day 29
Destroying Legal Rights

"Why are you so angry?" the LORD *asked Cain. "Why do you look so dejected?* [7] *You will be accepted if you do what is right. But if you refuse to do what is right, then watch out! Sin is crouching at the door, eager to control you. But you must subdue it and be its master."*
Genesis 4:6-7 NLT

I will never forget the moment I came into complete revelation of how I gave the enemy legal rights to wreak havoc in my life. At this point, I had already learned that I could tie God's hands concerning a matter. But I had no idea how one simple act could open the door for the enemy to come in. Long story short, God gifted me with a home that I now own. The Bible tells us that the blessings of the Lord maketh rich and added no sorrow. In my experience with God, this was more than true. Everything that God had ever blessed me with just keep on blessing me repeatedly as time went on, God's blessings truly "maketh rich." I like to think of it as a perpetual blessing. So, when it came to the house, any problem that would occur with it was quickly taken care of with no issues and no financial burdens. But, one day, I started having trouble with the heating system. The roof was leaking and I had a small kitchen fire with a pending insurance claim. I couldn't find a contractor to fix the roof for a reasonable price and I was low on funds. I hired someone new to fix the HVAC problem, but they left me with more problems and the HVAC still wasn't working.

So, I made a phone call to a contractor that I knew 'likes me' and wouldn't charge me for labor. To be honest, all I had to do was flash my pretty white smile and tell him he saved me, we never crossed any lines and we never dated. But things just got increasingly worse and more expensive. No insurance check, the roof is still leaking, and no heat for 2.5 months with no resolution in sight. One day I was so frustrated I began to pray, and I held God to his Word. I told him this house he had given me was causing me sorrow, and he needed to honor his Word that says his blessings added no sorrows. I understood that if he didn't, that would make him a liar, and my God was no liar. The Lord immediately responded and said Dennisha, my blessings do maketh rich and add no sorrows. But you are operating in a spirit of manipulation. You have opened the door and given legal rights to the enemy to mess with what I have blessed you with. The Lord explained to me that as soon as I decided to call the contractor who liked me and flashed my smile just so I wouldn't have to pay full price, that was the spirit of manipulation. I broke down in full repentance. The enemy had crept in unawares and it was all my fault. I immediately repented and asked God to forgive me and destroy the legal rights the enemy has to the house he blessed me with. Then I told the Lord I would not call that contractor back, but that he would need to lead me to a new contractor. God did that and more. After 2.5 months and almost $2000 later, within 48 hours of praying that one prayer, the roof was fixed for $130.00, the heat was fixed for $240, and I received three checks in the mail totaling over $10,000. Everything that I was struggling with concerning the house was taken care of in 48 hours just because I repented and destroyed the legal rights of the enemy.

We are spiritual beings living in a spiritual world governed by spiritual laws and every little sin gives the enemy legal rights to operate in our lives. Even telling a little white lie to maintain the secrecy of a surprise party can give the enemy legal rights.

When things are constantly going wrong in your life, and it seems like one bad thing keeps leading to another bad thing, it's wise to ask yourself did I open a door and allow the enemy to come in and wreak havoc in my life? Because the enemy is truly roaming around seeking whom he may devour, he is seeking legal rights. True repentance and forgiveness destroy legal rights. It's that simple. List all the legal rights you can identify in your life and ask yourself how willing are you to destroy them? Ask yourself this question, does the desire to have the life you envision outweigh your desire to not deal with certain issues? Forgiving others, including yourself, is imperative to your freedom. Forgiveness + repentance = freedom!

Day 30
Lacking Nothing

"Consider it pure joy, my brothers and sisters,[a] whenever you face trials of many kinds, ³ because you know that the testing of your faith produces perseverance. ⁴ Let perseverance finish its work so that you may be mature and complete, not lacking anything."
James 1:2-4 NIV

When it's all said and done, God wants that when he gives us what he has promised us, we will be perfect and complete, lacking nothing because he's a good father and all good gifts come from heaven. He wants to make sure we are fully equipped and prepared to fully enjoy the promise land that he is taking us into. One of my number one prayers is that God would fully shape, make, and mold me to be the wife he has called me to be according to his Word because I don't want to ruin a good thing. I don't want to be like the children of Israel who walked into the promised land and then ended up serving other gods drifting away from God and ending up in captivity, valuing the promise more than the God who gave it. I refuse to allow pride to trick me into believing that would never happen to me, causing me to skip the process and run ahead of God, blessing my own self before time. Before I am completely ready and graced to receive it and never lose it, allowing God to get all the glory. Because I want my life to be lacking nothing, I embrace the process God takes me through to be prepared for every promise that he has for me. Because they truly do "maketh rich and addeth no sorrow."

We have a tendency to be in such a rush to get what we want that we never take a moment to consider why God wants to process us before he releases the promise to us. We never take a moment to consider that we may be the reason why it's taking so long because we are not as ready as we think we are. Like a mom who really wasn't emotionally ready for her toddler to start school or a wife who wasn't ready for the season of depression that would hit her husband and now the marriage is struggling because she doesn't know how to comfort him. Or a couple with a great salary who never learned how to steward their finances well, so they weren't prepared for the recession and layoffs. God doesn't have us waiting just so that we can learn how to cultivate patience. We are also waiting so we can be perfect and whole, lacking nothing.

How many times have you heard wait upon the Lord? Or wait well? Wait well, might sound like a cliche but when you understand the purpose of the wait, you can embrace it, accelerate it, appreciate it, and thrive in it.

Don't just survive the waiting period. Thrive in it!

It's not God, it's me: take a moment to list all the things you are waiting on God for. What are some of the things he has promised you? One at a time, take each of these things to the Lord and ask him what he needs you to do or cultivate on your end in order to team up with him to see his promises come to pass in your life. Write down the Lord's instructions and obey them.

Author Bio

Dennisha N. Blake holds the title of an ordained prophet at the New Church of Signs and Wonders. Additionally, she is the CEO and founder of FaithInTheJourney LLC and Led by The Spirit Academy. As a kingdom strategist, life purpose coach, and accomplished public speaker, Dennisha has been recognized as a recipient of the prestigious 2023 Powerhouse Women with Purpose award.

With a decade of experience in ministry and a background in mission work, Dennisha channels her passion towards empowering Christian women. Her focus lies in guiding them beyond simply hearing the voice of God, enabling them to confidently execute His instructions without fear of the unknown. Through her work, Dennisha strives to make a positive impact on the lives of individuals and communities, empowering them to embrace their most abundant lives.

9 781915 930897